IN THIS ISSUE:

tour!sm TATTLER .com

ISSUE 01 JANUARY 2017

PUBLISHER
Tourism Tattler (Pty) Ltd.
PO Box 891, Umhlanga Rocks, 4320
KwaZulu-Natal, South Africa.
Website: *www.tourismtattler.com*

EXECUTIVE EDITOR Des Langkilde
Cell: +27 (0)82 374 7260
Fax: +27 (0)86 651 8080
E-mail: *editor@tourismtattler.com*
Skype: tourismtattler

MAGAZINE ADVERTISING
ADVERTISING DIRECTOR Bev Langkilde
Cell: +27 (0)71 224 9971
Fax: +27 (0)86 656 3860
E-mail: *bev@tourismtattler.com*
Skype: bevtourismtattler

SUBSCRIPTIONS
http://eepurl.com/bocldD

BACK ISSUES (Click on the covers below).

▼ DEC 2016	▼ NOV 2016	▼ OCT 2016

▼ SEP 2016	▼ AUG 2016	▼ JUL 2016

▼ JUN 2016	▼ MAY 2016	▼ APR 2016

▼ MAR 2016	▼ FEB 2016	▼ JAN 2016

CONTENTS

Front cover image courtesy of South African Tourism

EDITORIAL CONTRIBUTORS

Brett Hendricks
Chris Brown
Ian van Vuuren
Jeff Schmitz
Jennifer Nagy
Jeremy Smith
Juergen T. Steinmetz

Louis Nel
Martin Janse van Vuuren
Richard Bray
Taleb Rifai
Tine Brodegaard Hansen
Wolfgang H. Thome

MAGAZINE SPONSORS

I0478816

ACCREDITATION

Official Travel Trade Journal and Media Partner to:

The Africa Travel Association (ATA)

Tel: +1 212 447 1357 • Email: info@africatravelassociation.org • Website: www.africatravelassociation.org

ATA is a division of the Corporate Council on Africa (CCA), and a registered non-profit trade association in the USA, with headquarters in Washington, DC and chapters around the world. ATA is dedicated to promoting travel and tourism to Africa and strengthening intra-Africa partnerships. Established in 1975, ATA provides services to both the public and private sectors of the industry.

The African Travel & Tourism Association (Atta)

Tel: +44 20 7937 4408 • Email: info@atta.travel • Website: www.atta.travel

Members in 22 African countries and 37 worldwide use Atta to: Network and collaborate with peers in African tourism; Grow their online presence with a branded profile; Ask and answer specialist questions and give advice; and Attend key industry events.

National Accommodation Association of South Africa (NAA-SA)

Tel: +27 86 186 2272 • Fax: +2786 225 9858 • Website: www.naa-sa.co.za

The NAA-SA is a network of mainly smaller accommodation providers around South Africa – from B&Bs in country towns offering comfortable personal service to luxurious boutique city lodges with those extra special touches – you're sure to find a suitable place, and at the same time feel confident that your stay at an NAA-SA member's establishment will meet your requirements.

Regional Tourism Organisation of Southern Africa (RETOSA)

Tel: +27 11 315 2420/1 • Fax: +27 11 315 2422 • Website: www.retosa.co.za

RETOSA is a Southern African Development Community (SADC) institution responsible for tourism growth and development. RETOSA's aims are to increase tourist arrivals to the region through. RETOSA Member States are Angola, Botswana, DR Congo, Lesotho, Madagascar, Malawi, Mauritius, Mozambique, Namibia, Seychelles, South Africa, Swaziland, Tanzania, Zambia and Zimbabwe.

Southern African Vehicle Rental and Leasing Association (SAVRALA)

Contact: manager@savrala.co.za • Website: www.savrala.co.za

Founded in the 1970's, SAVRALA is the representative voice of Southern Africa's vehicle rental, leasing and fleet management sector. Our members have a combined national footprint with more than 600 branches countrywide. SAVRALA are instrumental in steering industry standards and continuously strive to protect both their members' interests, and those of the public, and are therefore widely respected within corporate and government sectors.

Seychelles Hospitality & Tourism Association (SHTA)

Tel: +248 432 5560 • Fax: +248 422 5718 • Website: www.shta.sc

The Seychelles Hospitality and Tourism Association was created in 2002 when the Seychelles Hotel Association merged with the Seychelles Hotel and Guesthouse Association. SHTA's primary focus is to unite all Seychelles tourism industry stakeholders under one association in order to be better prepared to defend the interest of the industry and its sustainability as the pillar of the country's economy.

Tourism, Hotel Investment and Networking Conference 2016

Website: www.thincafrica.hvsconferences.com

THINC Africa 2016 takes place in Cape Town from 6-7 September.

International Coalition of Tourism Partners (ICTP)

Website: www.tourismpartners.org

ICTP is a travel and tourism coalition of global destinations committed to Quality Services and Green Growth.

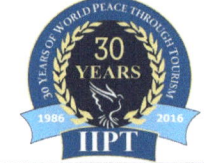

International Institute for Peace through Tourism

Website: www.iipt.org

IIPT is dedicated to fostering tourism initiatives that contribute to international understanding and cooperation.

World Travel Market

WTM Africa - Cape Town in April, WTM Latin America - São Paulo in April, and WTM - London in November. WTM is the place to do business.

The Safari Awards

Website: www.safariawards.com

Safari Award finalists are amongst the top 3% in Africa and the winners are unquestionably the best.

World Luxury Hotel Awards

Website: www.luxuryhotelawards.com

World Luxury Hotel Awards is an international company that provides award recognition to the best hotels from all over the world.

ICTP Statement:
Jordan & Berlin Terror Attacks

By **Juergen T. Steinmetz.**

On behalf of the International Coalition of Tourism Partners, I would like to extend our sympathy and condolences to the victims and their loved ones affected by the criminal attacks in Jordan, and in Berlin during December 2016. Both incidents were senseless acts by disguised criminals aimed at disabling the world's largest industry: Travel and Tourism.

In the Jordan incident, outlaws carried out an attack on a police station in the southern Jordanian city of Kerak, in the vicinity of the Kerak Castle. This cowardly attack killed 5 members of the security forces, a Canadian tourist and 4 gunmen. There were also 12 injuries reported as a result of this heinous act.

It took heroes like Jordanian law enforcement to prevent more harm, and it will take all of us, our community of travel and tourism professionals, to take leadership and encourage our clients and the public to consider travelling to amazing places including Berlin, Jordan, Egypt, Istanbul, Brussels, Nice, Paris, Kenya, Tunisia, and New York.

You may not see this in the headlines, but everything possible is being done in these great destinations and most other parts of the world to keep travellers safe.

Terror attacks make headlines, but we should not forget the proportion of criminal incidents a tourist could fall victim to, compared to a billion people travelling each year. The world, including those places that had been randomly hit by widely-publicized headlines, are safe and will remain safe.

In other places, criminal acts are becoming routine. Dozens are getting killed in Chicago every week by gunshots, and yet tourism, meetings, and conventions in the Windy City are booming.

Don't let a handful of fanatics and criminals alter our way of life. Travel and Tourism is a contributor to peace and understanding. Travel and Tourism translate to jobs and prosperity for 10% of the world's population. This makes our industry one of the largest economic players. Travel and Tourism must and will remain resilient.

In the Berlin incident, tourists from all over the world, and local "Berliners" alike, were enjoying the Christmas Market next to the famous Kaiser Wilhelm Memorial Church, when a truck ploughed into the market, injuring at least 48 people and killing 12 as a result. Police confirmed in a press conference to the German media that the incident was related to terror.

Berlin is a great city, and Germany will remain a welcoming country and a model for this troubled world. Islam is a peaceful religion. The same counts for Christianity, Judaism, Hinduism, Buddhism. Not believing in a particular God, doesn't mean believing in doing harm.

However, if you think hate and corporal punishment and randomly killing children, tourists, and old people attending a Christmas Market will get you to Heaven or Nirvana or the like, you will be in for a terrible reality. The reality is you are simply a criminal, and disrespectful of human life. t

---

About the Author: Juergen T. Steinmetz is the chairman of the International Coalition of Tourism Partners (ICTP) – a grassroots Travel & Tourism coalition of destinations and stakeholders. For more information on ICTP and how to join members in 131 countries without any cost, visit ictp.travel

New Year Message

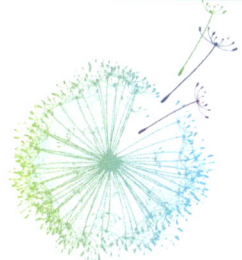

2017
INTERNATIONAL YEAR
OF SUSTAINABLE TOURISM
FOR DEVELOPMENT

Dear friends,

I write to you as I begin my final year as UNWTO Secretary-General, a position I have been privileged to hold for almost seven years at an Agency I have been proud to serve for the past decade.

During this time I have seen tourism become one of the world's most important and impactful socio-economic sectors of our times. I have seen its growing relevance to the lives of millions around the world, to the preservation of our common values and to greater understanding among people of all walks of life.

I have seen increasing commitment from the international community, with many countries realizing the potential for tourism to become a pillar of their development. This commitment is attested to by the inclusion of tourism in the universal 17 Sustainable Development Goals (SDGs) agreed upon by 193 nations in 2015.

And now I am very privileged and grateful to be celebrating 2017 as the International Year of Sustainable Tourism for Development. The UN General Assembly's decision to dedicate 2017 to tourism's contribution to sustainable and inclusive growth was no coincidence. Tourism is increasingly and rightly being recognized as a sector that can help usher in a better world.

2017 is a unique opportunity for us to promote the contribution of tourism to achieving the future we want – and also to determine, together, the exact role we will have tourism play in the sustainable development agenda, to and beyond 2030.

Of course, many challenges remain before our sector. Yet if there is one thing I will always remember from my time in this captivating and rewarding sector, it is that tourism is a sector of hope. Not only is it one of the most resilient economic sectors, but it also unites people across backgrounds, cultures and continents every day. Through travel, we gain understanding, tolerance, and empathy for our fellow man – essential in the globalization era, where our global village can only prosper through harmonious living.

The tremendous hope that our sector provides should inspire us all to act for the good of people and planet. Together we can be the change we want to see.

Let us all remember that whatever we do in life; our core business is to make this world a better place.

I wish you a very happy International Year of Sustainable Tourism for Development 2017.

Taleb Rifai

Secretary-General, World Tourism Organization (UNWTO)

SAA Museum Society

If cultural, heritage or nostalgia tourism are niche sectors that your business focusses on, then the South African Airways Museum Society (SAAMS) is definitely worth including in itineraries. Here's why.

By **Des Langkilde**.

Conveniently positioned on a tract of land adjacent to Rand Airport's runway 29 in Germiston, Gauteng, South Africa, the SAAMS displays an impressive collection of Static Display Aircraft.

Included in the display are two Boeing 747s, "Lebombo" which flew over Ellis Park at the 1995 Rugby World Cup and a rare Boeing 747SP named "Maluti". There is also a B747 "Classic" Simulator and an Airbus A300 Simulator, both, sadly, no longer operational. "Lebombo" is open for viewing, just not the cockpit. For interior access to any of the other static display aircraft an application must be made via e-mail, stating the number of visitors. Ideally

at least a week's notice is required to give the SAAMS sufficient time to allocate a Tour Guide.

Three of the aircraft that the museum currently owns are serviceable; two Douglas DC-4 Skymasters and a Douglas DC-3 Dakota. These aircraft are all classic propeller-driven airliners that started their careers in the mid 1940s and still ply their trade carrying tourists to exotic destinations in Southern Africa. The aircraft are leased to Skyclass Aviation who operate them on charter work, including film shoots and scenic flights around Johannesburg and environs. SkyClass holds a Part 121 certificate with both Domestic and International licences

and has gained an enviable reputation and is well known and respected among local and overseas tour operators for their African air tour safari excursions. Clients fly into the Johannesburg hub and from there make their way to various destinations using the SkyClass aircraft. The airliners can depart out of Rand Airport, Lanseria Airport or from OR Tambo International Airport. Popular destinations include National and Private game parks within and outside of South Africa, sporting weekends and holidays, corporate trips, flying safaris to such exotic places as the Victoria Falls, Chobe Game Lodge, the Islands off Mozambique and beyond up into Northern and Eastern Africa and Zanzibar.

▼ *An aerial view of the aircraft display. Founded in 1986, SAAMS is a non-profit volunteer organisation collecting and preserving the history of civil aviation in South Africa.*

▼ *The SAAMS Simulator and Radio Room houses a rare Air Trainers Limited AT50 Jet Instrument Flying Trainer – a licensed built "Link Trainer" circa 1954.*

▼ *A Lockheed L18-08 Lodestar.*

Photo's courtesy of SAA Museum Society, John Austin-Williams and Bruce Perkins of Flight Zone.

ZS-ABI , a de Havilland DH60G Gipsy Moth (1934). Typical of photos that can be found in the SAA Museum Society Archives.

Display Hall

The SAAMS display hall is located in the Transvaal Aviation Club (TAC) building situated on the eastern side of Rand Airport. Historic items such as photographs, aircraft models, crew uniforms, aircraft instruments, timetables and small artefacts of SAA and general civil aviation memorabilia are on display. Visitors are welcome to take photographs inside the display hall. There is also a series of SAA Museum aircraft posters (450x310mm) with history and technical specifications produced by The Aviation Shop with original artwork by Pierre Lowe Victor.

Ian Carrol Library

Over the years, the SAAMS has amassed a wonderful collection of aviation related books, technical manuals, historical documents, photographs, magazines and historic footage. The material in the library is available for research purposes.

Museum Shop

The SAAMS Shop carries a wide range of aviation related items, that will appeal to both young and old. Items include: T-Shirts, Magazines, Books, Toys, Aircraft Models, Caps, Badges and DVDs.

Refreshments

There is a delightful restaurant inside the old Transvaal Aviation Club, TAC, building. A variety of scrumptious meals are available and there is a playground area for children.

One of the Rand Airport taxiways passes directly in front of the complex and affords aircraft spotters and photographers a choice spot.

Model Aircraft

For collectors of scale model aircraft, both plastic snap-fit and die-cast, SAAMS have created a web page dedicated to models of SAA aircraft. Click here to view.

Photo Archive

An impressive collection of historical photographs can be found on the SAAMS website. The images are free to share provided that the pictures are credited to individual photographers. Click here to view. t

Contact Details:

Address:	Transvaal Aviation Club building, Dakota Crescent, Rand Airport, Germiston, Johannesburg.
GPS:	-26.241799, 28.159343 or -26° 14' 30.48", +28° 9' 33.63"
Open Hours:	Tue to Sun 09h00 to 15h00 Public Holidays: 09h00 to 15h00. Closed Mondays, 25 December and 1 January.
Entrance Fee:	R35 (adults), R25 (children).
Tel:	+27 (0) 76 879-5044
E-mail:	info@saamuseum.co.za
Website:	www.saamuseum.co.za

▼ The museum has a lovely paved area with braai facility and tables with umbrellas and seating for up to 50 people. The museum is available for corporate-related functions, conferences, product launches, ceremonies and school outings.

▼ The museum houses an extensive collection of airline artefacts and memorabilia.

SPONSORED FEATURE

WiFi at Safari Lodges:
a Key Influencer?

By **Des Langkilde**.

A Big Five safari is all about the sightings and experiences. Sharing the thrill of these experiences with friends and family on social media is what travellers do. But internet connectivity at game reserves can be sporadic, if available at all. So how important is WiFi access as a key facility to influence traveller destination decisions?

In days gone by, recording these sightings and experiences on film or video enabled the safari goer to re-live the safari again and again. The cost of photographic equipment usually meant one camera per couple or family. The relatively recent developments in digital photography and social media channels have made every safari-goer a photographer, often with multiple devices being able to photograph and record every aspect of the safari. Sharing the thrill of these safari experiences with friends and family on social media channels has become the norm.

But internet connectivity at game reserves can be sporadic, often with poor bandwidth, which makes for frustrating experiences when tech-savvy safari goers want to engage with the outside world.

One would think that the whole point of an African safari is to get away from it all - to get back to nature, and leave technology behind! So just how important is WiFi access? Is it a factor when travellers make their destination decisions? Do properties with great connectivity benefit more than those with poor or no connectivity?

Looking at traveller booking and experience-sharing behavioural patterns, connectivity does seem to be important:

- TripAdvisor's 'TripBarometer 2016[1]', shows that 56% of travellers share their experience with pictures on Tripadvisor reviews, 50% on Facebook, and 24% on Instagram.

- As a decision-making influencer, a recent 'Tourism For All' survey[2] conducted by SA Tourism shows that 53% of travellers get their inspiration from travel websites and blogs.

Given these stats, it's clear that internet access is important to travellers. In South Africa, most 4-5 star lodges offer WiFi in rooms or in communal lodge areas, either complimentary or for a small charge.

Looking for specifics, I turned to Vernon Wait, Marketing Director of Lalibela Private Game Reserve in South Africa's malaria-free Eastern Cape province.

"Meeting the needs of guests is a priority at Lalibela. To this end, we have recently significantly upgraded the bandwidth of our WiFi service in the lodges (Lentaba Lodge, Tree Tops and Mark's Camp). And whilst we never did charge guests for WiFi, they used to have to enter a WiFi code in order to access the internet. We have done away with this so guests' devices now automatically connect to our high-speed internet as soon as they arrive at their lodge.

"Obviously, the WiFi range does not extend across the entire 10,255 hectares (over 25,000 acres) of the reserve, so guests may not be able to connect to the internet while on a game drive, but then one would hope that they are more engrossed in taking pictures of the Big Five, which they then upload to their social media platforms after returning to the lodge." says Wait.

An innovative idea launched at Lalibela Private Game Reserve encourages guests to share their images on social media with a hashtag.

Caught in action at Lalibela are the Taylor-Smiths from the UK who stayed at Lentaba Safari Lodge, the #lalibelasafari frame makes an ideal prop for focussing on the camp fire at Tree Tops Safari Lodge, and field guide Thembani Gcayiya (affectionately known as Tim) with the Feil's from Germany.

Talking about social interaction, does providing complimentary internet access affect the natural ambience of the lodge? I asked Rob Gradwell, Managing Director of Lalibela.

For example, while reviewing a lodge in Kenya recently I noticed a family of four sitting in the main lodge area with their attention glued to their respective smartphones and tablets. For over an hour, not a word was uttered between them.

"How guests choose to spend their leisure time is obviously not for me to comment on, but we do try to encourage guest interaction as we believe this forms part of the overall safari experience. There is a balance that needs to be maintained – the need for guests to connect when they want to and the need for guests to relax and to be able to get away from it all.

"Some people's idea of relaxing is to sit on the internet and interact on social media whereas others have chosen a safari in the bush to get away from that! The dining rooms at each lodge, for example, have large tables where guests dine together rather than at separate tables, which does encourage conversation among guests. It would detract from the ambience were some guests to sit at the dining table and remove themselves from the group by being on their phones or tablets.

"We believe that providing broadband WiFi access has become an essential hospitality

The Hartwells from the USA pose with field guide Siya Mandabana prior to a game drive.

facility," says Gradwell. "The jury is out at Lalibela – we have currently decided to only have internet connectivity in our lodges and not in the rooms, but should it be the other way round? Should it be only in the rooms and not in the lodges? What about having it in both? There is no right or wrong answer and I would ask the travel trade to please engage with us with their thoughts as we ponder this conundrum."

So there you have it – straight from the horse's mouth (or should that be zebra's mouth?), and backed up by research – WiFi access has become an essential hospitality facility, and does influence traveller destination decisions, specifically when combined with interactive marketing initiatives to encourage guests to share their images on social media, such as the #lalibelasafari prop.

But the conundrum faced by Gradwell is one that I'm sure many game reserve executives are pondering.

What are your thoughts on the subject? [t]

---

1. https://d2bxpc4ajzxry0.cloudfront.net/TripAdvisorInsights/sites/default/files/downloads/2750/tripbarometer_2016_full_report_-_04_oct_2016_-_st12.compressed.pdf

2. http://welcome.southafrica.net/uploads/files/TourismForAll_Infographic.pdf

Market Intelligence Report

The information below was extracted from data available as at **09 January 2017**. By **Martin Jansen van Vuuren** of **Grant Thornton**.

ARRIVALS

The latest available data from **Statistics South Africa** is for **January** to **October 2016***:

	Current period	Change over same period last year
UK	354 292	11.7%
Germany	237 740	22.6%
USA	286 857	17.5%
India	81 429	26.7%
China (incl Hong Kong)	98 645	53.7%
Overseas Arrivals	2 021 305	19.7%
African Arrivals	6 239 022	12.7%
Total Foreign Arrivals	8 269 707	14.3%

HOTEL STATS

The latest available data from **STR Global** is for **January** to **October 2016**:

Current period	Average Room Occupancy (ARO)	Average Room Rate (ARR)	Revenue Per Available Room (RevPAR)
All Hotels in SA	64.5%	R 1 155	R 745
All 5-star hotels in SA	65.1%	R 2 115	R 1 376
All 4-star hotels in SA	64.1%	R 1 069	R 685
All 3-star hotels in SA	64.8%	R 915	R 593
Change over same period last year			
All Hotels in SA	3.0%	8.9%	12.1%
All 5-star hotels in SA	5.1%	10.8%	16.4%
All 4-star hotels in SA	3.8%	6.5%	10.6%
All 3-star hotels in SA	3.3%	6.2%	9.7%

ACSA DATA

The latest available data from **ACSA** is for **October 2016**:

Change over same period last year	Passengers arriving on International Flights	Passengers arriving on Regional Flights	Passengers arriving on Domestic Flights
OR Tambo International	2.9%	4.4%	5.5%
Cape Town International	13.6%	22.6%	6.3%
King Shaka International	20.9%	N/A	8.9%

CAR RENTAL DATA

The latest available data from **SAVRALA** is for **January** to **May 2016**:

	Current period	Change over same period last year
Industry Rentals	1 134 620	-1%
Industry Utilisation	74.2%	3.6%
Industry Revenue	2 375 892 450	10%

WHAT THIS MEANS FOR MY BUSINESS

The data continues to indicate the recovery of both the foreign leisure and domestic business market. The outlook for 2017 is cautiously optimistic. The settling of the effects of events such as Brexit and the USA elections and the improvement in economic growth in South Africa's main foreign sources markets should aid the growth in foreign tourism to South Africa. South African politics and the slow economic recovery will dampen growth in the domestic leisure and business markets. It should be kept in mind that tourism growth in 2016 was on top of a dismal 2015 and although growth in tourism is expected, the high growth rates experienced in 2016 is unlikely to be repeated in 2017. *Note that African Arrivals plus Overseas Arrivals do not add to Total Foreign Arrivals due to the exclusion of unspecified arrivals, which could not be allocated to either African or Overseas. t

For more information contact Martin at Grant Thornton on +27 (0)21 417 8838 or visit: http://www.gt.co.za

Image Attribution: World Economic Forum / Eric Miller - Creative Commons license.

Stakeholders Lack Confidence in
Tanzanian Tourism Minister

"The meeting with our Minister was a shambles," ranted a regular Arusha-based stakeholder before adding "He got no grip on the industry, he does not understand tourism and his insistence earlier in [2016] that tourism must be subjected to VAT shows that he is against the industry he is supposed to represent in government."

"He is another in a long line of failures which shows government does not appreciate the sector at all. One of the few over the past years of substance was Kagesheki but most others were just posturing peacocks" – leaving out some of the most unprintable comments made on the subject.

Prof. Jumanne Abdallah Maghembe, the current Minister of Natural Resources and Tourism for the United Republic of Tanzania, met industry representatives over government demands of a $2,000 licence fee, irrespective of the size of the company in question, and for some time banned the entrance of tour vehicles into the parks, unless the drivers carried copies of the licences with them. This led to widespread protests from a large number of small safari operators, almost all owned by Tanzanians, who tried to carve out a niche in the market for themselves by going independent.

By **Prof. Dr Wolfgang H. Thome**.

Participants in the meeting then reported that the minister had to make a humiliating climbdown and suspend the measure, allowing tour vehicles into the parks for the time being, while a more moderate and measured solution was sought.

At the same meeting, the government also came under fire for not doing enough to promote and market the country, again leading to some feeble excuses by the minister, who failed once more to embrace the private sector's challenges and problems and – like with his stand on VAT – only served to further estrange himself from the sector.

The minister reportedly left red-faced after a barrage of discontent by meeting participants with TATO (Tanzania Association of Tour Operators) representatives mincing no words how detrimental the government's measures were for the entire industry.

Said another regular source in a volunteered statement, given on condition of anonymity for obvious reasons – considering the current crackdown on any form of dissent: "The sooner they recognise that a good working relationship between government and the private sector is absolutely essential, the

better. This minister has failed us, full stop. We feel like we are all treated like tax evaders and cheats until proven innocent and that is not climate under which the sector can prosper. Maghembe should be the first to make way for a better-suited person because tourism deserves the best, not a recycled politician who has done nothing else but offend us".

Harsh words no doubt, but by the look of it, quite understandable. t

This article appeared first on eTN: Global Travel & Tourism News

Editor's Note: In 2016, Maghembe faced international controversy after allowing a company back into Tanzania that he knew had committed dozens of wildlife crimes. The company – Green Mile Safari from the United Arab Emirates – had been kicked out of Tanzania after their own promotional video showed animal torture and repeated violations of Tanzania law. Maghembe's decision to let the company back in was widely assumed in news reports to be based on his acceptance of a bribe from Green Mile. Perhaps it's time for President John Magufuli to move Maghembe back to his old post as Minister of Agriculture, Food and Cooperatives where his degree in Forestry would be more appropriate.

About the Author: Prof. Dr Wolfgang H. Thome is the publisher of ATC News, and a regular contributor to TourismTattler, eTurboNews and The Travel Group. With over 40 years of experience in the tourism, aviation and conservation fields in Kenya, Tanzania and Uganda, Thome covers all aspects of safari operations, hotel operations and air operations.

Social Impact Initiative
ETHIOPIA

Valerie Bowden, the author of 'Backpacking Africa for Beginners', has an inspiring story to tell. And it's not about her book. It's about a snack made from Teff and a business that she plans to use as a social upliftment initiative aimed at creating jobs for marginalised Ethiopians.

By **Des Langkilde**.

Before delving into Valerie's story, though, we need clarify what teff is. According to Wikipedia, *Eragrostis tef* is a species of lovegrass native to Eritrea and Ethiopia. The word *"teff"* is connected by folk etymology to the Ethio-Semitic root *"Iff"*, which means "lost" (because of the small size of the grain). The US National Research Council characterised teff as having the "potential to improve nutrition, boost food security, foster rural development and support sustainable land care."[1]

In Ethiopia, teff is used to make *injera* whereby the seeds are fermented for 3-4 days before it is cooked as pancakes or sun-baked to create *dirkosh* - a crispy snack with a mildly sour or bitter taste.

And this is where Val's story comes in.

"Although I was born and raised in Fort Wayne, Indiana I've called Ethiopia home for the past two years. During my time here, I transitioned to a plant based, low fat, vegan lifestyle, which has changed my health dramatically. One thing I miss though is [kettle fried] chips. I think chips and dip are everybody's favourite snack. But for me finding a chip that was low fat and didn't have oil in it was impossible. That's when I stumbled upon dirkosh as the perfect option. It's so delicious and filling at the same time," says Val.

She discovered from an article published in the Washington Post that 'one serving of teff offers 7 grammes of protein, 4 grammes of dietary fibre, 25% of your daily recommended magnesium, 20% of your daily iron, and 10% of your calcium, vitamin B6, and zinc [requirements].'

Armed with this knowledge Val started to experiment with her own unique recipe that lessened the time of fermenting and created a more suitable flavour for foreign taste buds. After a few tweaks, she made it lighter and crispier resulting in the perfect snack.

So what's in her recipe? "I use just a few ingredients. In fact, maybe it's better to begin by listing what's not in Dirkosh. It's oil, preservative, chemical, and gluten free. So Dirkosh is all natural, low-fat, vegan goodness. Besides teff, just a pinch of volcano salt is added. Even our flavoured Dirkosh chips only have a few added

local spices. Nothing you can't pronounce or find in a typical Ethiopian kitchen is in our snack," says Val.

After meeting, falling in love, and marrying her then neighbour Alula Kibrom, the couple set about turning their newly created 'Dirkosh Crunch' product into a business with export potential.

"One of the reasons I wanted to take my new passion for plant-based foods into a business is because of the social impact we can have in Ethiopia. I actually have a master's degree in social work and after living here I noticed that creating jobs in a conscious capitalism kind of way is one of the best ways to make a difference", says Val.

"Now that I am aware of teff's benefits, I think everyone in the world should have access to it. They might not like eating it the same way Ethiopians do, but they can enjoy it in different recipes. For example, a lot of people in the West like crunchy foods. That's why we adapted dirkosh to make it into a crispy snack that more people would want to eat," adds Alula.

Social Impact

Embracing their love for Ethiopia, Val and Alula plan to put a unique fact about Ethiopian culture onto the packaging of each new batch of Dirkosh Crunch.

"Why? Because stereotypes matter, and it's time for this country's image to be updated. More than that, though, we want to create sustainable jobs, which is what African countries, including Ethiopia, need to move out of poverty. Experts believe that Ethiopia has more agricultural potential than most countries in the world, yet they profit little. Why? Because even if a farmer produces a crop that can be sold to Western countries, it is sold in bulk and processed and packaged outside. This creates little impact on the community.

"Dirkosh is different. Everything, including the processing and packaging, will be made within our community using local skills. And to be honest, there are not a lot of great options for packaging currently available within the country. That amount gets even smaller when we focus on making it green friendly and up to international standards," says the entrepreneurial couple.

1. *National Research Council (1996-02-14). "Tef". Lost Crops of Africa: Volume I: Grains. Lost Crops of Africa.*

Business Funding

Val and Alula's Dirkosh Crunch concept has been accepted into the Growth Africa Accelerator Program, beating almost 100 start-ups in Ethiopia to become one of the twelve finalists chosen for Growth Africa's first Ethiopian Cohort. They are now receiving six months of business and marketing training, and the opportunity to become investment ready.

To get the business started for local production, a crowd funding site at Gofundme.com was set up and the couple used the first tranch of $3000 to hire their first workers.

"When we first set off, we said we wanted to provide jobs for at-risk women. Then we hired Tarikua. Tarikua is funny, sassy, caring, and hard-working. But she never had a job because physically she's put together differently than others. I wish I could have captured the look in her eyes when she was handed her first paycheck ever. For the first time in her life, she can provide for herself. But hiring Tarikua made us realise something important. She doesn't want to be defined by her challenges. And she earns her job. So we decided that we no longer "give" jobs to those with disabilities. But we do give a fair chance to anyone who wants to work, an opportunity to try. And our hope is to keep our workforce 90% full of women or those who were previously overlooked for employment an opportunity to be a part of our Dirkosh Crunch family.

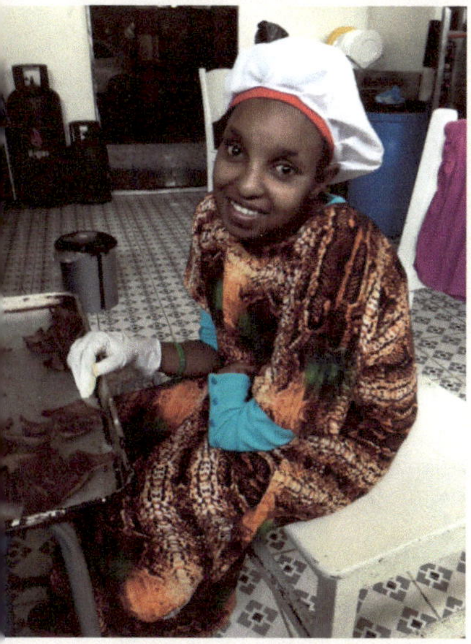

"Almost everybody has told us to move production of Dirkosh to Europe or the US or anywhere else but Ethiopia. But we believe that the future of Africa depends on being internationally competitive. No developing country has moved out of poverty by charity or donations. It's become sustainable, prosperous, and healthy because of JOBS.

"If African farmers could grow crops that are produced and processed in their local countries, they would create food and prosperity for their people and the world! We're talking about kids getting medicine, food, and going to school because their parents can provide!

"That's what Dirkosh Crunch is all about. A sustainable future for Ethiopia that will inspire more agri-processing on the continent.

"But there is a gap. In order for us to register the company legally in Ethiopia, and get it ready for grants and investors, we need to invest $50,000 USD. Which we don't have," says Val.

In conclusion, if there are any angel investors or NGO heads reading this article who would like to fill this missing gap, Val is more than willing to sign contracts or provide financial statements showing that money is going where it is intended to go.

For more information visit www.eatdirkosh.com or to make a donation visit www.gofundme.com/dirkosh

Funds raised from the sale of her e-book 'Backpacking Africa for Beginners' will be ploughed back into the business.

Watch the video - click on the image

GOOD SERVICE

Seeds Future

TOURISM GROWTH

By **Brett Hendricks**

These days, travellers do not vote only with their feet when dissatisfied with the quality of service they receive. They also vote with their fingers, sharing stories of their experience with friends and posting messages on social media.

Millennials, in particular, have become accustomed to rating everything – accommodation, transport, food and beverages. And the potential for an incident of poor service to be captured on video and end up trending on social media is huge, with damaging consequences for the business.

But this cuts both ways.

When people receive excellent service, they often share this among their friends and social media channels, potentially influencing them to try out the experience, be it a new restaurant or a visit to another country. They also leave glowing reviews on travel advice websites such as TripAdvisor and Lonely Planet.

More tourists have been visiting South Africa this year than last, with large growth being posted in visitors from Asia and the Middle East. These overseas visitors travel thousands of kilometres and spend large sums of money to come to our country, and rightly expect that they will be welcomed warmly and treated to a memorable experience.

Delivering high-quality service, therefore, should be our number one priority. And if we get it right, it will serve as the base for future growth in tourism as a whole. This is especially important for businesses in long-haul destinations such as South Africa because one bad experience can dissuade a potential traveller from making the investment in time and money to travel such a great distance.

Often, whenever the topic of service quality is brought up, a common response from tourism businesses is that we do not have the right calibre of people working in the sector. Or that the country has a shortage of skills.

This is true to some extent. But service excellence is not something we are born with. It has to be taught – and skills have to be developed.

Tourism employs large numbers of unskilled or low-skilled people, and their work affects the quality of the customer experience. It is in our best interests as businesses to see the investment in up-skilling such people as an investment in the future profitability of the tourism sector and our own businesses. That simple change to how we think about it will put us in a frame of mind to treat investments in training and skills development as we would any other investment.

That is to say that we should expect it to generate some kind of future economic or financial return. And we should have in place the systems to monitor the performance of our training and skills development programmes so that we can make changes if the outcomes are not what we anticipated.

I have seen some excellent training and skills development programmes, especially in the hospitality sector. Many of these are run by large tourism businesses that have the resources to invest in such programmes. I would like to see businesses that run effective programmes develop partnerships with smaller tourism businesses to help them up-skill their employees.

The tourism eco-system in this country is such that no business, no matter how big, can claim to be completely immune from the effects of poor service elsewhere in the value chain. As I said earlier, one bad service experience can put off a traveller from returning to the country, or from recommending that others visit, with knock-on effects for every tourism business in South Africa.

We want the tourists who will be visiting our shores in 2017 to come back again. We want them to become ambassadors for tourism in South Africa. And the only way we can do this is if we ensure that their entire stay in the country is the best and most worthwhile that it can be. 🔳

***About the Author: Brett Hendricks** is the General Manager of the Thebe Tourism Group. For more information visit Thebe.co.za*

Note: South African Tourism has a Welcome SA website filled with resources to help make your guests' stay a memorable one. A free module-based online learning programme is also available to equip your staff with the skills to better sell South Africa as a tourist destination. There are two courses: SA Specialist: Essentials and SA Specialist: Experiences. For star-graded hospitality establishments, the Lilizela Tourism Awards programme provides recognition for service excellence, while the TGCSA's Basket of Benefits provides free tips, legal advice, and procurement discounts. **Editor.**

Livingston Supply Company

**The Social Media Competition has been discontinued.
Watch this space for new reader incentives in 2017.**

Congratulations to our December 2016 Social Media competition winner:

Jacis Lodges at **Madikwe Game Reserve** has been selected as our final winner. **Jacis Lodges** will receive **2 Kenyan Scarfs** with the compliments of **Livingstones Supply Co – *Suppliers of the Finest Products to the Hospitality Industry***.

Winner

@jacislodges Jacis Lodges offers African safaris and honeymoons, friendly service and exceptional game viewing. perfect for romantic safaris and yummy fire cooked meals under African skies!
For more information visit www. jacislodges.co.za

These beautiful scarfs are made from 100% Viscose. Size: 35 x 160 cm. Produced locally in Kenya from imported fabric in a range of exquisitely woven patterns, the vibrant and rich as well soft and muted colours reflect the beauty and ethnicity of the African nature and culture. These scarfs may be worn to temper the evening or morning chill or to keep cool in the African sun. Adding elegance, style, comfort and functionality to any wardrobe.

For more information visit www.livingstonessupplyco.co.za

OPEN LETTER

China's Wildlife Crimes in Namibia

In this Open Letter to China's Ambassador Xin Shunkang, Dr Chris Brown, CEO of the Namibian Chamber of Environment, demands that the Chinese government takes responsibility and leadership in addressing the illegal trade in wildlife and commits to stopping all wildlife crimes perpetrated by its nationals in Namibia.

Dear Ambassador Xin Shunkang,

During the past month, several Chinese nationals have been apprehended and charged with wildlife crimes, including illegal possession of rhino horn, ivory and pangolin skins and scales.

Your embassy is on record stating that "it will not allow a few of its nationals who have been arrested in connection with poaching to tarnish its country's image."

While we recognize that not all Chinese nationals are involved in wildlife crimes, Namibia's environmental community believes that the situation regarding Chinese nationals committing wildlife crimes in Namibia is far more serious and broad-based than you have acknowledged.

The fact is, unless effective action is taken now to halt wildlife crime, your country will get an increasingly bad name. And you and your country are best placed to address the problem.

Until the arrival of Chinese nationals in significant numbers in Namibia, commercial wildlife crime was extremely low. As Chinese nationals moved into all regions of Namibia, setting up businesses, networks, acquiring mineral prospecting licenses and offering payment for wildlife products, the incidence of poaching, illegal wildlife capture, collection, killing and export has increased exponentially.

Driving our country's wildlife to extinction

Chinese nationals have been involved in, and/or are the commercial drivers behind:
- the escalating poaching of rhinos and elephants in Namibia and the illegal export of rhino horn and ivory,
- the capture, trade and export of pangolins,
- the import of Chinese monofilament nets in industrial quantities via Zambia to the northeast of Namibia, which are destroying the fisheries of the Zambezi, Chobe, Kwando and Okavango Rivers,
- the unsustainable commercialization of fisheries in these north-eastern rivers and wetland systems for export to cities and towns in neighbouring countries,
- the capture and killing of Carmine Bee-eaters at their breeding colonies by means of nets,
- the rise in bush-meat poaching wherever Chinese nationals are working on road construction and other infrastructure, including tortoises, monitor lizards, pythons and any other form of wild meat, including from protected and endangered species,
- the illegal collection of shellfish on the Namibian coast,
- the illegal transit through Namibia and attempted export of poached abalone from Cape waters through Namibian ports.

We are also aware of long-standing interests by some Chinese nationals to start a shark fin industry in Namibia, a practice that has caused widespread damage to shark populations in many parts of the world, including in South Africa.

And more recently, Chinese nationals have proposed to capture marine mammals and seabirds for the Asian aquarium market. The Namibian scientific and environmental communities have strongly rejected this proposal on sound conservation and ethical grounds, as has the Namibian public.

We are concerned by an apparent total disregard by some Chinese nationals for Namibia's wildlife, conservation, and animal welfare laws and values. Namibians are proud of their environmental heritage, their rich wildlife resources and the institutional mechanisms that are in place to sustainably manage them.

Namibia as a nation has worked hard to protect and nurture these natural assets. Namibia's wildlife management provides an international example for good conservation and sustainable use. We have not made these investments so that some Chinese nationals, or anyone else, can pillage them.

Adding insult to injury

The illegal commercial interests of some Chinese nationals towards Namibia's protected wildlife has exploited the vulnerability of poor Namibians and divided societies. It undermines local ownership of natural resources and the empowerment of communities to managing their wildlife wisely, for long-term communal benefits. It undermines Namibia's globally acclaimed Community-based Conservancy programme, and it does considerable damage to Namibia's international conservation and sustainable development reputation.

The recent announcement by the Chinese business community that it is contributing N$30,000 to counter rhino poaching, while acknowledging that Namibians are deeply concerned about the situation caused by some Chinese nationals, totally fails to understand the economic scale of the problem. Indeed, it is an insult to the environmental sector in Namibia and to Namibia's environment.

An initial very conservative estimate of the extent of the losses to Namibia's wildlife and ecosystems caused by Chinese nationals is about N$811 million. And this does not include the significant additional resources that Namibia's government, donors, communities, private sector, and NGOs have had to commit to combat escalating wildlife crimes. These funds should rather have been spent on more productive activities such as continuing to develop the wildlife and tourism sectors to improve the lives and livelihoods of rural communities.

We do not claim to fully understand the relationship between Chinese nationals and the Chinese state. It appears that Chinese nationals are not at liberty to obtain passports and travel independently around the world, bringing their personal capital and starting businesses in their own names in whatever country would have them, independent of the Chinese state.

As such, Chinese nationals in Namibia appear to be part of a state supported system. So, as the highest ranking Chinese official in Namibia, we would expect all Chinese nationals in Namibia to fall under your authority.

As such, we now call on you to put an immediate stop to the illegal wildlife crimes perpetrated, encouraged, funded, incentivised or otherwise committed and supported, by some Chinese nationals in Namibia.

And now, please help us to repair the damage caused!

Further, we call on the Chinese government to make good, by investing in Namibia's environment sector in a transparent and internationally recognized manner, and in proportion to the damage caused, to help rebuild Namibia's wildlife populations, ecosystems, management systems and reputation.

This letter does not represent only the views of the 40 environmental organisations listed below, but also represents the views of countless members of the Namibian public and our international friends.

The sentiments expressed in social media over the past months, from across a broad spectrum of Namibian society, and their outrage at the leading role that Chinese nationals play in wildlife crime have surely been noted by you and members of your embassy.

You will also be aware of the sentiments expressed by our President, by the Minister of Environment and Tourism, and by the Namibian Police Inspector General as reported in the local media. The time for inaction is over.

China has a policy of non-intervention and yet these actions by some Chinese nationals, and the apparent inaction of your embassy to address the problem, are direct and indirect interventions that have disastrous impacts on our policy and legal framework, on our environmental culture and ethics, on our natural heritage and on our national conservation and development programmes. They also have huge negative impacts on our people and their livelihoods, and on our international reputation.

In late 2014 the out-going US President Barack Obama, in an interview with the New York Times, accused China of being a "free rider" for the last 30 years in not taking on more of its international obligations. In the last couple of years, particularly under the

leadership of your President Xi Jinping, China has taken a decidedly more active leadership role in global issues. It is time to extend that leadership to natural resources and in particular, to wildlife conservation.

Indeed, the Chinese philosopher Zhuangzi, almost 2,000 years ago, may have been amongst the first to advocate for ecological sustainability within a philosophy of coexistence between man and nature. If China is to live up to its stated aims of having positive interactions between peoples and countries then this, for us in Namibia, is a critical issue.

Time for China to take responsibility!

We support our government's policy of attracting foreign investment to stimulate growth, employment and development. And we counter all forms of xenophobia and profiling. However, we expect foreign investors and their nationals to abide by Namibia's laws, and to embrace Namibia's cultures, ethics, and values.

Too many Chinese nationals have abused Namibia's environmental laws, and this is causing growing resentment and anger amongst Namibians. By their criminal actions, some Chinese nationals have drawn attention to themselves and their nationality through their blatant disregard of Namibia's legal and environmental values. We are also concerned at how little action the Chinese embassy in Namibia appears to be taking to address the problem.

We as concerned Namibian Environmental NGOs and businesses, who it should be stated, are pro-sustainable use, stand ready to work with a China that willingly takes on greater responsibility and leadership in addressing the illegal trade in wildlife and, in particular, commits to putting an immediate stop to all wildlife crimes in Namibia by its Chinese nationals.

Yours sincerely,

Dr Chris Brown, CEO, Namibian Chamber of Environment.

Namibian Chamber of Environment members:

African Penguin Conservation Project
Africat Foundation
Cheetah Conservation Fund (CCF)
Desert Elephant Conservation
Earthlife Namibia
Eco Awards Namibia
Edu Ventures
Environmental Compliance Consulting
EnviroScience
Frank Bockmühl
Giraffe Conservation Foundation
Jaro Consultancy
Naankuse Foundation
Namib Desert Environmental Education Trust
Namibia Animal Rehabilitation, Research & Education Centre (NARREC)
Namibia Nature Foundation (NNF)

Namibia Scientific Society
Namibian Association of CBNRM Support Organizations (NACSO)
Namibian Hydrogeological Association
NamibRand Nature Reserve
Ongava Game Reserve
Otjikoto Environmental and Education Trust
Progress Namibia TAS
Research and Information Services of Namibia
Southern Africa Institute for Environmental Assessment (SAIEA)
Save The Rhino Trust (SRT)
Scientific Society Swakopmund
Sustainable Solutions Trust (SST)
The Namibian Environmental and Wildlife Society
Tosco Trust
Venture Publications

Other Namibian Environmental Organisations supporting this letter:

Botanical Society of Namibia
Brown Hyena Research Project
Gondwana Collection Namibia
Game Rangers Association of Africa (GRAA) – Namibian Chapter
Integrated Rural Development and Nature Conservation (IRDNC)
Kavango Open Africa Route (KOAR)
Legal Assistance Centre (LAC)
Namibia Bird Club
Wilderness Safaris - Namibia

This article has been published with acknowledgement to the Namibian Chamber of Environment and The Ecologist.

RÉUNION ISLAND

The Ultimate Nature & Leisure Destination

Covering an area of more than 2500km² and the largest island in the Mascarene archipelago, Réunion Island is an Indian Ocean destination you don't want your tourism clients miss out on.

The island enjoys a fair tropical climate, resulting in lush vegetation, abundant greeneries with nearly half of the total area of Réunion Island classified as World Heritage Site by UNESCO. Réunion Island is the perfect place for discovery, diverse sceneries, a vibrant culture and thrilling activities and is like a treasure island with amazing natural jewels waiting to be discovered!

Le Piton de La Fournaise

Le Piton de La Fournaise is one of the most active volcanoes on the planet and probably the greatest treasure of Reunion Island. The volcano is the most visited place on the island and the most thrilling attraction. This volcano can be visited by helicopter or microlight planes, but the best way to discover the volcano is the hard way, trekking!

Trekkers on the summit of Le Piton de La Fournaise

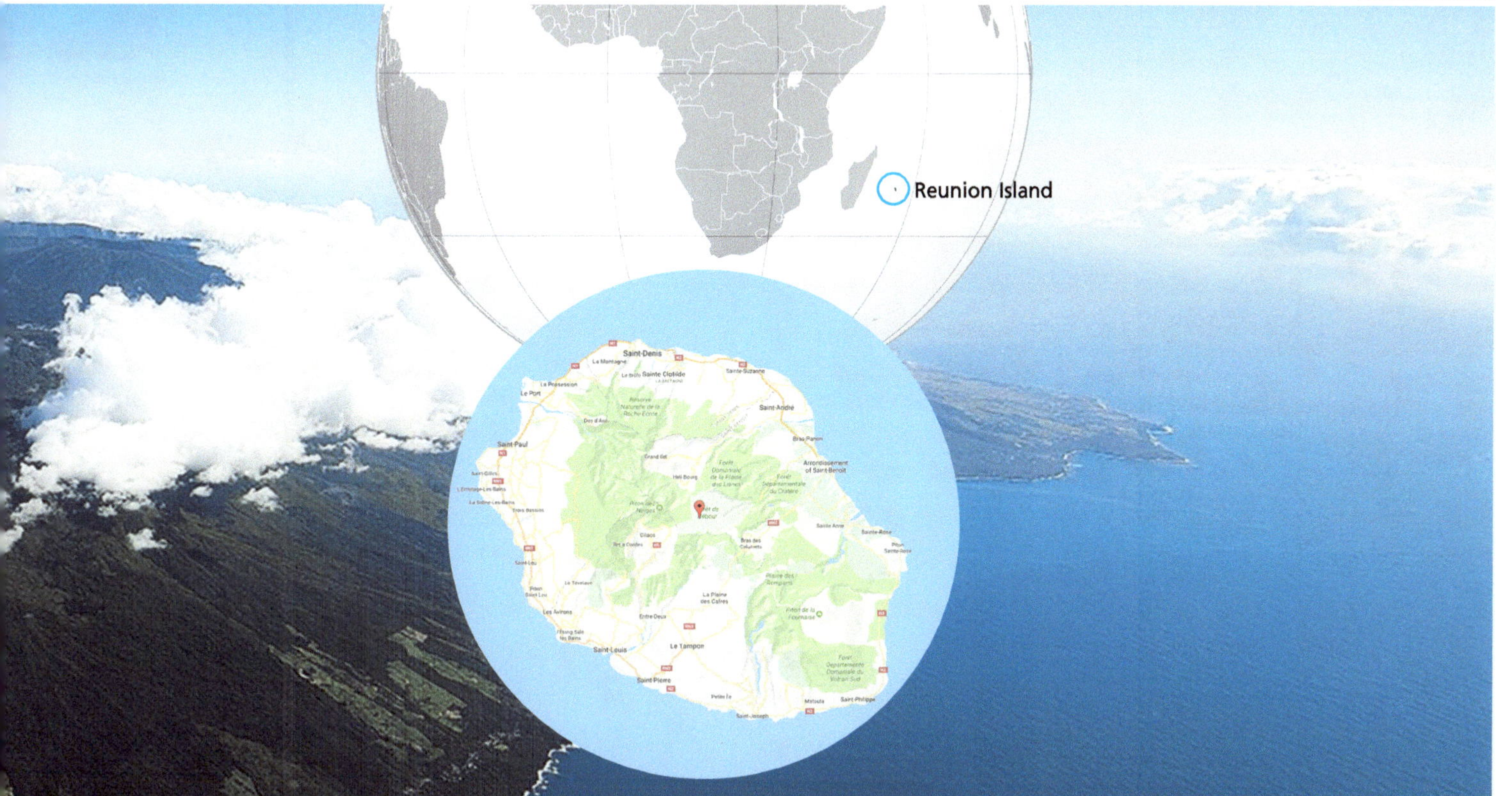

Reunion Island

Quick facts

Réunion Island, a French department in the Indian Ocean, is known for its volcanic, rainforested interior, coral reefs and beaches. Its most iconic landmark is Piton de la Fournaise, a climbable active volcano standing 2,632m (8,635 ft.). Piton des Neiges, a massive extinct volcano, and Réunion's 3 calderas (natural amphitheaters formed by collapsed volcanoes), are also climbing destinations.

Currency: Euro

Capital: Saint-Denis

Population: 843,617 (2015)

Voile de la Mariée

A waterfall whose water cascading resembles that of a veil of a bride? Only on Réunion Island! *Voile de la Mariée* is one of the many natural treasures of Réunion Island and is truly a marvel to behold.

Garden of Eden

The Garden of Eden, or rather Eden Garden of Réunion Island is a beautiful botanical garden of 2.5 hectares which includes more than 700 species of plants. You will discover a wide variety of tropical fauna and flora including some endemic species of the island. Even though it is located at the heart of the town of Saint-Gilles, Eden garden is one of the quietest places in the city.

There is so much to see and do on the island, gaze at the scenery, or laze at one of the lagoons, enjoy authentic Réunionese food and dance, visit the St Paul Market or simply relax! However your clients choose to spend their time, prepare them to be in awe!

Click here to visit the Réunion Island blog for special packages to this gem in the Indian Ocean. 🇹

Réunion Island Tourism Board is represented in South Africa by Atout France.

The Voile de la Mariée waterfalls

The Garden of Eden

Unpacking
STAR GRADING

What exactly does the term "star graded" mean and what is the significance of such a rating for hoteliers and their guests?

By **Richard Bray**.

In a nutshell, the Tourism Grading Council of South Africa (TGCSA) has a set grading criteria and minimum standards by which accommodation establishments are rated from one-star to five-star.

These guidelines ensure local establishments uphold their allure as international travel destinations.

Contrary to what it may seem, a one-star rating for instance does not mean a hotel is of a lesser quality. It simply means that there are additional requirements needed to progress to a rating of two-star and upwards.

According to Mina Monare, Consumer Feedback Liaison Officer at the TGCSA, a grading can be changed at a later stage, depending on circumstances. This could either be in the form of a downgrade in star grading level or an upgrade whereby an establishment is reconfigured (through renovations) to meet minimum requirements and standards for a higher star grading level.

She adds: "Star grading in South Africa is voluntary. There are just on 5 300 star graded establishments in the country, a true testament of the star grading system's value to both tourism operators and travellers."

Hotels that are eligible for grading are, according to the TGSA website, establishments that provide 'formal accommodation with full or limited service to the traveling public'. In addition, they have a reception area and offer a dining facility. They must have a minimum of four rooms as well.

The entry requirements for all star ratings by the TGCSA include that an on-site representative must be contactable seven days a week, 24 hours a day.

The website further stipulates that where applicable, any meal(s) and beverages must be provided from outlets within the boundary walls of the property, which may or may not be operated by the property. Servicing of rooms seven days a week must be included and a formal reception area must be provided. Bathroom facilities must be en-suite.

Additional requirements for four-star and five-star ratings include onsite parking with security for guests, a valet service, room service, a concierge, porterage and luggage handling, as well as other services such as baby and child minding, message passing, and newspaper delivery. Full housekeeping and laundry services must also be provided.

By way of example, Premier Hotels & Resorts have several properties in their three-star and four-star categories. These hotels are definitely reaping the many rewards of being star graded, which include exclusive access to the Basket of Benefits - a plethora of tailor-made offerings ranging from discounted procurement and amenities to training and development service providers along with market access.

In conclusion, I quote Monare: "Graded establishments enjoy access to business from the government as only graded establishments can be used by government officials. They have exclusive rights to display the globally-recognised plaque – giving establishments an immediate quality identity." t

About the Author: Richard Bray is the Group Operations Manager for Premier Hotels & Resorts. A born Hotelier, with over 30 years of experience in the hotel and restaurant industry, Richard studied Hotel Management at the Wits Hotel School and holds a Postgraduate Diploma from the University of Pretoria. For more information visit www. premierhotels.co.za

Five Steps to a Successful Towel & Linen Reuse Scheme

Hotel approaches to towel and linen sustainability vary considerably. Here are five simple steps to getting it right.

Image courtesy of Aman Resorts - Sri Lanka

By **Jeremy Smith**.

1: Use The Most Environmentally Friendly Materials Possible

W Hotels in North America have launched a new range of bed linen made from recycled plastic bottles. Early May saw the hotel launch the Ekocycle range of bedlinen, designed in a partnership between Will.i.am from the Black Eyed Peas, and Coca Cola. Each king size Ekocycle sheet contains around 31 recycled 600ml plastic bottles. It's an excellent example of making sustainability seem cool while designing waste out of a system.

2: Get Your Message Right

Too often hotels print exaggerated greenwash messages on their cards, suggesting that people can somehow 'save the planet' by using less towels. Increasing amounts of research show this form of messaging isn't the most successful approach. Researchers at the University of Luxembourg arranged for hotels in two Swiss and Austrian ski resorts to put three different signs in their bathrooms: one was a typical request to use fewer towels to help the environment; one said that 75 per cent of hotel guests reuse their towels; and the third claimed three-quarters of guests in that particular room reused their towels. The third approach was by some margin the most successful, backing up earlier research that came to the same conclusion. "People want to be accepted into groups and so we act in ways that make us belong," wrote the study's lead author Dr Gerhard Reese in The Journal of Social Psychology. "Instinctively, we feel close to those who have used a hotel room before us, believing that they are similar to ourselves. Thus we are more likely to follow their behaviour."

3: Show A Tangible Benefit For Guests

Starwood's 'Make a Green Choice' scheme give guests a $5 food and drink voucher or 500 Starwood points for every day they decline housekeeping's services (except departure day). of course this approach not only rewards guests, it does so by driving custom to its own restaurants. However as a word of warning about unforeseen negative consequences, in December 2014, 200 protesters amassed outside Toronto's Sheraton Centre objecting that the green programme was taking away jobs. Working out how to reassure staff that their jobs are not at risk from sustainability schemes that will by their nature reduce their workload will be a challenge for any accommodation provider looking for a truly integrated solution.

4: Show A Tangible Benefit For Someone Else

Radisson Blu has just launched a new towel reuse campaign with water charity Just a Drop. For every 250 towels that guests reuse, the hotel chain will donate enough money to Just a Drop to provide clean water for a child for life. Guests will learn how many children were provided with drinking water through the hotel's in bathroom cards, with Radisson Blu hoping to ensure 12,000 children have access to fresh drinking water each year.

5: Don't Just Throw Towels And Linen Away

At the Eco Fashion Week Show, seven designers showed off kimonos made from former bed linen from the local Fairmount Waterfront Hotel. Likewise, Marriott is partnering with a UK social enterprise called SleepingBags to repurpose hotel bed linen that has reached the end of its life back into items that can be used in guest rooms – such as bathrobes, tote bags and slippers.

Know of any other innovative responses to the hotel linen reuse scheme? Share them on Twitter at @wtm_wrtd

---

About the Author: Jeremy Smith is a writer and consultant specialising in responsible tourism, and author of Clean Breaks – 500 New Ways to See the World (Rough Guides). Many interesting articles can be found on Jeremy's blog at http://jmcsmith.co.uk/category/blog/

Hotel Study Reveals Plans for
ATTRACTING GUESTS

Improving guest experience through technology spurs 74% of hotels and resorts to implement location-based technologies to tailor services.

By **Jeff Schmitz**.

Results of the recently released global Zebra Hospitality Vision Study – a body of research that analyses the hotel industry and trends in travellers' preferences and technology requirements that affect their overall satisfaction – found that changes in consumer expectations for fast WiFi, helpful guest assistants and loyalty rewards have prompted the hospitality industry to invest in technology that enhances the guest experience and provides added convenience for smartphone check-in, location-based offers and services and digitally-enabled loyalty programmes.

The hospitality industry is becoming an increasingly competitive market, especially with the proliferation of niche hotels and home rental websites.

To continue to attract and delight guests, hotels and resorts are making significant technology investments to enhance hotel services. This includes enabling guests – 92% of whom carry a smartphone – to use their smartphones to do everything from ordering food to receiving text alerts on room readiness and possible upgrades.

Although the impact of technology varies by market, digital disruption is changing the way hotels and guests interact in every region. Zebra will continue to deliver guest engagement and staff effectiveness solutions to better serve guests.

KEY FACTS

Wider WiFi access

To help move staff to mobile computers for more guest interaction, expand location services for guests and deliver reliable wireless access, 77% of hotels/resorts surveyed worldwide are expanding WiFi coverage. 66% of guests report they have a better experience when associates use the latest technology and 68% of guests expressed a desire to use their smartphone to speed up check-in.

Customised offers and loyalty programmes

Nearly three-quarters (74%) of guests surveyed appreciate hotels that customise messaging and offers, and 75% are willing to share personal information, such as gender, age and email address, in exchange for tailored promotions, coupons, priority service or loyalty points.

Location-based services

To create highly customised offers and perks, 74% of surveyed hotels/resorts are planning to implement location-based technologies within the next year – prioritising guest recognition and analytics, geo-targeted mobile offers and special promotions and upgrades. The study shows guests are less comfortable sharing their location than their personal information, though attitudes differ among generations. 34% of Millennials are comfortable sharing their current location compared to 13% of 50- to 64-year-olds.

Regional findings

Guest recognition is the top driver for location technologies in North America where travellers are least concerned about sharing their location and social media profiles and most willing to use self-service technology.

Hotels/resorts in Latin America are moving fastest to implement location-based technologies where guests also have the highest expectations for receiving personal attention from hotel/resort assistants.

In the Asia-Pacific region, offering special promotions and geo-targeting mobile users are the top drivers behind implementing location technologies where guests are influenced most by helpful guest assistants to stay at a hotel/resort.

Survey Background and Methodology

Nearly 1,200 hotel and resort workers in IT, operations, marketing or guest services and more than 1,680 consumers were surveyed in two separate global studies. The first study focused on the hotel/resort industry's views on guest needs, strategic technology and service plans and vision for the future. The second study measured travellers' preferences, technology requirements and opinions on the factors influencing their overall satisfaction at hotels and resorts.

About the author: Jeff Schmitz is the Senior Vice President and Chief Marketing Officer, Zebra Technologies Corporation (NASDAQ: ZBRA), a global leader in providing solutions and services that give enterprises real-time visibility into their operations. www.zebra.com

 **ZEBRA**

HIGH TECH FOR HIGH TOUCH

2016 EUROPEAN HOSPITALITY VISION STUDY

IGNITING GUEST INTERACTIONS

Harnessing the power of consumers' mobile devices is a vital component of the hospitality industry's technology renaissance

KEY QR CODE APPLICATIONS
1. Check-in reservation confirmation
2. Website for local events/restaurants
3. Access to surveys/reviews
4. Coupons
5. Loyalty points
6. Identity scanning
7. Mobile payment

61% of hotels in Europe are implementing QR code applications within the next year

The hospitality industry is courting today's ever-connected guests with a high-tech-for-high-touch game plan. According to Zebra's European Hospitality Vision Study, hotels and resorts are tapping technology to ease, enrich and personalize the guest experience.

Learn more at
www.zebra.com/hospitality

AUTOMATING CONVENIENCE

Increasing technology usage to expedite mundane processes and service guests better

57% of guests want to use technology to speed up getting what they want

 ROOM 224 IS READY FOR YOU.

HOTEL/RESORT PREFERENCES
- Smartphone check-in
- Room preferences based on profile
- Personalized guest greetings upon arrival

PERSONALIZATION

Differentiating the guest stay via unique personalized experiences to strengthen loyalty and encourage repeat visits

67% of guests appreciate customized messaging and offers

GUEST PREFERENCES FOR PERSONALIZATION
- 84% Want room selected based on personal preferences such as window location, room location and bed configuration
- 69% Would like rooms pre-stocked with preferred amenities before arrival
- 69% Want room to automatically adjust thermostat based on preference
- 57% Interested in using smartphones and tablets to control in-room needs (TV, restaurant/spa reservations, local events, room service)

TOP FACTORS INFLUENCING GUESTS STAYS

 WELCOME, MR. MARTIN. ENJOY YOUR STAY.
PERSONALIZED INTERACTIONS

HELPFUL GUEST ASSISTANTS

 LOYALTY
LOYALTY PROGRAM/ REWARDS

LOCATION TECHNOLOGIES

Making special offers based on preferences and locations such as step-by-step directions and reservation reminders

HOTEL/RESORT PRIORITIES FOR LOCATION-BASED TECHNOLOGY
1. Guest recognition
2. Special promotions/upgrades
3. Notification of arrival/check-in
4. Customer/guest analytics
5. Geo-targeted mobile offers

60% of hotels plan to implement location technologies within the next year

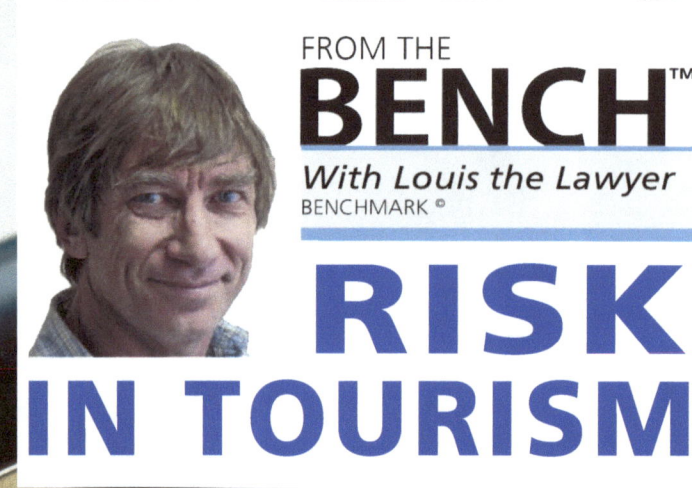

FROM THE
BENCH™
With Louis the Lawyer
BENCHMARK ©

RISK IN TOURISM

THE LAW: CONTRACTS

- Part 25 -

The Role of:
Service Level Agreements

Disputes: You Don't Have To Go To Court!

As suggested in my article on standard terms and conditions last month, *'A further relevant clause could provide for alternative dispute resolution ('ADR'). Disputes are traditionally resolved by summons and ensuing court cases, but ADR was initiated in the '80s and has become quite popular. There is the more commonly known arbitration and then the lesser know mediation. These forms of ADR have the benefit over litigation of being less costly (by and large), more private, and quicker'* – I promised you a more detailed article, so here it is!

Locally ADR in the travel and tourism industry takes place on a very informal and ad hoc basis. It has not been formalised but I personally believe such a step is necessary if not overdue as more and more disputes are arising in the industry, either by virtue of disgruntled travellers or between members of organisations such as ASATA, EXSA, FEDHASA, FGASA, SAACI, SACIA, SATSA and SITE. I have, with the help of ASATA and SATSA promoted and conducted (largely successful I am glad to be able to add!) a few such ADR sessions, mainly based on very informal mediation with the parties presenting themselves (i.e. no legal representation). However, I am really keen to formalise the procedure and to get 'buy-in' from all the associations mentioned above for the reasons discussed below. The best way to do this would be to make it an integral part of membership by including it in the constitution.

What is the situation internationally in the travel and tourism industry? ABTA ('The Association of British travel Agents') *'..has got together with the Chartered Institute of Arbitrators (ClArb) to help agents and operators resolve legal disputes with minimum hassle'* by providing a *'.. .new commercial mediation and arbitration scheme for tour operators and travel agents'.* IFTTA (The International Forum of Travel and Tourism Advocates – an international organization for lawyers, advocates and educators who specialise in travel and tourism law – of which I am a member) has forged links with the world Travel Dispute Center, Inc. and the Travel Dispute Mediation LLC (based in Florida, USA) to *'conduct ADR seminars and*

serve as the central mediation assignment center for graduates of the ADR seminars which it conducts' – So, if we want to 'tap into' overseas expertise, it is 'ready and waiting'!

These innovative steps by ABTA and IFFTA raise a few questions: What in fact is arbitration? What is mediation? Will either actually result in 'minimum hassle'? Is it cheaper and/or more effective than litigation or other mechanisms available in South Africa for the resolution of disputes?

Let's start by looking at definitions of arbitration and mediation: *'Arbitration is a private judicial hearing with an outcome that binds the parties and puts an end to the dispute between them'* (as defined by the Arbitration Foundation of South Africa ('AFSA' – see below). *'Arbitration is the reference of a dispute to an arbitrator for determination in a judicial manner after hearing both parties'* (Ken Douglas of Webber Wentzel 1986)

Mediation, on the other hand, is a form of Alternative Dispute Resolution ('ADR') and is chosen by parties who would *'.. rather settle their dispute amicably, with the help of a third person, but without being bound to the outcome'* (The Association of Arbitrators)

Confusing? Yes, I'm sure so let's confuse you some more. The aforementioned are two ways in which parties can resolve disputes, but there are more.

In Part 26 (Feb 2017) I'll take a brief look at the others before we focus on arbitration and mediation, the options chosen by ABTA.

This series of articles explores the legal aspects associated with the risks of operating an adventure tourism business, with specific relevance to the legal framework applicable to South Africa.

Part 7

By 'Louis The Lawyer'

Image courtesy of Canopy Tours

ADVENTURE TOURISM
from a legal perspective

Summary

Part 1 provided definitions for the term Adventure, while **Part 2** looked at risk in terms of Nationality of Participant, Service Providers, Bookings, and Terms & Conditions, and **Part 3** covered Indemnity and Requirements of the CPA. **Part 4** explained why signage must go in hand with a sound indemnity and waiver form, **Part 5** dealt with Duty of Care in relation to Negligence, Omission, and Relationship, and **Part 6** concluded Duty of Care with Acceptance of Risk and Insurance.

RISK IDENTIFICATION & MANAGEMENT CHECKLIST FOR ADVENTURE SPORT OPERATORS

Many, and probably most, of the adventure sport activities in South Africa are provided by businesses that specialise in their field, are passionate about it, are sound in terms of risk management, and have a good track record. On the other hand there are no doubt operators who supplement their own services with that of third parties, and then there are those travel and tourism businesses who do not actually carry out or provide the services it offers to its clients ('pax'/'participants') itself but 'farm out' the entire process to a third party service provider ('SP').

Legally speaking it means that the operator acts as the principal where it provides the service itself and where SP is involved, it could still be acting as the principal but mostly it will be acting as an agent, facilitator, broker or as referred to in the Consumer Protection Act ('the CPA'), an 'intermediary' – the latter has changed the liability landscape not only as far as imposing substantial obligations on the operator but adding to it the matter of absolute liability. (More about this later).

This article is aimed at all adventure sport operators, no matter in which guise it transacts business ('the Business') and in a manner of speaking, it is a guideline to ensure that the exposure of the Business is identified and dealt with as effectively as possible. It pertains not only to such SP but also to the Business itself – some introspection and audit of its own systems is required and should be an annual prerequisite.

I will not go into much detail about the different types of entity, save to say that the Business can be e.g. a sole proprietor, partnership, close corporation, company or trading trust. Each of these has its own idiosyncrasies but given the nature of the activities adventure sport entails, I would strongly advise against the first two as liability is effectively personal and the owner(s) can lose everything they own in the event of a catastrophe! Add to this cocktail the highly publicized and prevalent 'Duty of Care' issue (see Parts 5 and 6 of this series) and you may end up with a hangover of note!

It is imperative that your terms and conditions ('T&C') stipulate the capacity in which you are acting i.e. principal or agent or broker. This has very important legal, accountability and liability implications. It is not uncommon that the T&C states that all services provided by a SP will be subject to the SP's terms and conditions ('SP T&C') and that the contractual relationship will be established (regarding such services) directly between the SP and pax.

However such a clause has various implications and has, will, and may, give rise to problems. The Business may have a problem with European Community ('EC') pax and agents who will cite the EC regulations. (More about that later).

I have also (and more so recently) experienced cases where pax (or agent on behalf of the pax) refuses to sign the T&C containing such a clause and/or call for the SP T&C. This is now their right in terms of the CPA and the Business must provide it or provide access thereto.

There are also confidentiality implications - not only from a common law point of view, but also in terms of the Protection of Personal Information Act ('POPI') in so far as information is shared with third parties, whether locally or overseas (More about this later).

To be continued in Part 8.

Promoting
DOMESTIC TOURISM

Through their support of Fikile Hlatshwayo's book 'Blacks Do Caravan', South African Tourism aims to inspire families to travel. The book encourages South Africans to visit local destinations and to discover the therapeutic nature of camping along with the inherent beauty of the country.

BLACKS DO CARAVAN

Fikile Hlatshwayo

PUBLISHER: Jacana.co.za | ISBN: 978-1-4314-2377-4 | GENRE: Travel
FORMAT: Paperback | SIZE: 245x168mm | EXTENT: 180pp

Image courtesy of Grootbos Private Nature Reserve

TOURISM FOR ALL

The theme of universal accessibility was linked to the national campaign of #Tourismforall – South African Tourism's contribution to the UNWTO global theme for World Tourism Day 2016 – an initiative geared towards enabling all South Africans to enjoy travel opportunities in their own country.

Universal accessibility not only talks to the need to ensure that establishments can accommodate persons with disabilities but it also considers socio-economic factors. This basically comes down to how those who are hindered in some way shouldn't disregard travel in any way, be it a disability, age, or budget, everybody deserves to explore this beautiful country.

According to Hlatshwayo's book 'Blacks Do Caravan', her travels took her to over 60 caravan and camping parks across the country, a mode of travel she'd never considered before, where she discovered that caravan camping can be used as a tool to unite South Africans.

"I learnt many things during this journey. Most importantly was about how close a camping community can be and how people look out for one another. This was a life-changing and enriching experience for me and my family.

"In a caravan park there is no sense of fear, no walls and all security features. There is a sense of belonging, connectivity with your inner self and, of course, the liberation nature has to offer," says Hlatshwayo.

The therapeutic nature of camping discovered by Hlatshwayo was that when she started this trip she was diagnosed with excessive 'burnout'; a condition that has become prevalent in this country due to work pressure, among other things. While on the trip she found fulfilment and healing.

She appealed to the Ministry of Tourism specifically to do more in promoting such camping adventures, which can also be a job creation tool.

Caravan camping is one of the most affordable forms with which to enjoy a holiday or short break. "Camping is very cheap and gives one access to all the 'hotspot' holiday destinations in South Africa. Many people do not know that there are campsites in Kruger National Park where a couple pays R250 a night for a campsite. Now, this is worth it! Money that is saved from accommodation can then be used for activities to entertain loved ones," Hlatshwayo concludes.

Another partnership initiative undertaken by South African Tourism is Gogo's on Tour, specifically designed to provide elderly people the opportunity to travel to local destinations and enjoy the beauty of South Africa, its people and vibrant culture.

Furthermore, the partnership will help improve the livelihood of approximately 1000 senior citizens from all nine provinces, from October 2016 until the end of March 2017. This further enforces South African Tourism's vision to create an accessible tourism environment in South Africa, and to subsequently contribute to the economic development of the country. t

Go to www.shotleft.co.za to find great destinations to visit all over South Africa!

PR VS Advertising

There's a misconception held by many business owners that public relations (PR) and advertising are completely interchangeable (in terms of the benefits that they offer), but that isn't true. While each has benefits, there are many reasons that PR is more effective for start-ups – especially for those in the hospitality industry.

By **Jennifer Nagy**.

Here are six examples of when using PR will be more effective than advertising for hospitality start-ups:

When you need to educate your audience

One of the most exciting things about working in the hospitality industry is the innovation that you experience firsthand. The difficult thing about being the company that is selling an innovative, new product is that it is necessary to educate your potential clients on why this product is different/better than others available in the market. Because many of these products are so technologically advanced, this can be a very arduous process – and a confusing one for your audiences. That's where PR comes in.

In conjunction with content marketing, PR is the best tactic to educate your potential customers and establish the company as an expert. It is possible to do this because hotel trade publications will publish vendor-neutral articles (articles that don't reference/sell a specific brand/product) that will teach hoteliers how to improve their operational processes. Over time, this exposure will help your company to sell your solution more effectively and significantly shorten the sales cycle.

When you want consumers to try out your product

A good way to provide media incentives for publishing your content is to offer the publisher the opportunity to give away a free trial of your product to their readers. By allowing the publication to manage the giveaway, it helps to increase their value to their audience, which will strengthen their readership, while giving your product valuable exposure.

When you want to create a stronger relationship with your target audience(s)

The public is accustomed to seeing ads everywhere – and distrusting the messaging that they see reflected in these ads. If you want your public(s) to have a positive impression of your company and/or products (and increased trust in purchasing from you), PR is a better approach; articles written about your company by a journalist - an independent third-party expert - gives your company more credibility in the mind of potential customers. The same message delivered by an advertising spokesperson may be ignored by many potential customers.

In addition, advertising is only effective at telling your audience your message, making it a one-way marketing tactic; in contrast, PR is a two-way communication tactic (communication flows from the brand to the audience and also in reverse), which makes it more appealing to potential customers and, therefore, more effective.

When you want to sell your product's story, not just your product

The inherent nature of a start-up (it's something new and different!) creates a story angle that will be of greater interest, and therefore, you are more likely to secure media coverage.

Especially when your product is re-thinking the industry's standard way of executing a task, there is a really interesting story behind its development; consumers love to read these stories, so media love to publish them.

When are you are on a budget

Traditional marketing tactics (such as billboards, TV commercials and radio ads) are less cost-efficient than PR. For example, a press release only needs to be distributed to media once (if you have a strong angle) and it will be picked up in numerous publications, on- and off-line, over time. This gets your message and product/service ongoing attention without an ongoing financial investment – unlike advertising, which requires you to continue paying for the advertisement to earn ongoing exposure.

Even more importantly, the results that can be achieved using PR (if executed properly), greatly exceed the ROI that can be earned from advertising.

To create or maintain your company's reputation, especially during a crisis

Establishing and maintaining your reputation is the essence of PR. As previously mentioned, having a journalist write about your company or product establishes a sense of credibility with readers/viewers.

In addition, during and after a corporate crisis, audiences are not as receptive to traditional advertising. By using PR to communicate with audiences (don't forget to apologize!) during a crisis, the company can mitigate the negative effects and more effectively protect (or rebuild) their reputation.

About the author: Jennifer Nagy is the President of JLNPR Inc – a full-service public relations and marketing agency that lives and breathes all facets of the travel technology industry.

To find out more about JLNPR visit www.jlnpr.com or contact Jennifer at jenn@jlnpr.com

Predictions: Native Ads in 2017

No one knows exactly what the future holds. However, the 23 outstanding experts (featured in the new e-book) have a better shot than most people at predicting how the coming year will affect native advertising. Reading their predictions, there's no doubt it will be a seminal year.

Reaching the right audiences on the right platforms is no easy task in a fragmented media landscape. Hopefully, the wise words of these 23 experts will contribute to making your work with native advertising even more successful in 2017.

Tine Brødegaard Hansen
Editor-in-Chief, Native Advertising Institute

Native Advertising definition: Paid content that matches a publication's editorial standards while meeting the audience's expectations. Facebook and Twitter fail this definition because neither are publishers. The same is true with Google AdWords. Source: www.copyblogger.com

Advertisers and publishers will focus on better quality.

Largely up to now branded content has been seen as a separate entity which is there to communicate a marketing message, rather than inform and entertain an audience. Brands and audiences will increasingly demand content which is compelling and resonates with them or they will vote with their feet, by using Ad Blockers or not engage with the content. Branded content will become as good or better than a publisher's normal editorial output by increased investment, a more integrated approach and a developing market where publishers have more confidence to control the execution.

Pete Wootton
Managing Director of Digital, Dennis Publishing

Marketers will realise that connecting with consumers through content is better

Smart brands now know that when consumers engage with their content, they engage with their brand. Content drives more impactful engagement with consumers and ultimately greater ROI on media spend than traditional display advertising does. With marketers increasing focus on content marketing, they will turn to native as a key content distribution strategy.

This shift will continue in 2017 as budgets increasingly move away from traditional display and toward native. According to eMarketer, native ad spending will grow at double-digit rates for several years, reaching $36.3 billion by 2021.

Lon Otremba
CEO, Bidtellect

Brands will take advantage of publishers' in-house content studios

In 2017, I expect to see brands take more advantage of in-house content studios at publishing companies as a couple of factors collide: more budget for direct marketing will go to Facebook and Google and scaling amazing content will get harder for brands to do internally. The brands that take advantage of in-house content studios will see a huge lift in sentiment and exposure, while the brands that rely only on one or two channels for direct sales will likely see ROI only increase in direct correlation with their on-platform spend. I also expect to see publishers to make sure that the demarcation of native advertising is clear.

Clare Carr
VP of Marketing, Parse.ly

For more insights download the free e-book at:

http://offers. nativeadvertisinginstitute. com/23predictions2017

TOURISM SECURITY
A Comparison on Safety Tips

By Ian van Vuuren

Project Consultant, Tourism Safety Initiative, Tourism Business Council of South Africa

Like many other tourist destinations in the world, it could be argued that South Africa has some way to go to manage the trade-off between providing information to travellers about safety and security considerations versus the important task of growing tourist numbers into the country.

The country's climate, scenery, infrastructure, its friendly people and a positive exchange rate all contribute to make South Africa a very attractive tourist destination. And with the visa debacle now behind us, there is virtually nothing that stands in the way of increasing tourist arrivals into the country.

Or is there? Safety and security is always upheld as our Achilles' heel, but if that is the case, why is a country like Thailand still welcoming more tourists than South Africa as a tourism destination? Could it be due to amongst other things, the way they deal with matters of safety and security?

One possible answer is that it could have to do with how safety and security matters are communicated and integrated into their marketing strategy. In a country like Thailand, despite having a much poorer safety and security record regarding tourist than South Africa, they are expecting 33 million tourists this year, which will be more than double the number to visit South Africa. And in a recent article the Thailand government has vowed to improve the situation, so no attempt is made at hiding the facts.

Looking at the selection of South African websites that deal with Tourism Safety (see analysis graphic alongside), and how they communicate regarding matters of safety and security, what lessons can be learned?

Firstly, one has to acknowledge that this is but the tip of the iceberg when it comes to tourism safety and security advice. Virtually every hotel and accommodation facility will have some advice or warning mechanism in place, be it electronic, brochures, z-folders, or even verbal warnings. The same also goes for every local municipality, especially within tourism dominated areas. This study therefore does not profess to be exhaustive.

There are a number of common themes that run through these safety tips. In most cases they deal with the various places where a tourist may find herself in the "travel value chain", i.e. at the airport, in the vehicle, on the street, at the accommodation facility, at places of leisure/attraction.

In most cases emergency numbers are provided, and in some cases also a list of embassy numbers.

Only in a few instances is information provided on card fraud prevention – this despite the fact that this is one of the major crimes affecting tourists (with ATM scams).

A few sites deal with how to positively identify members of the SAPS, by implication suggesting this may be a problem.

There is limited information on dealing with safety issues, as opposed to security, i.e. illnesses, malaria, wild animals (granted, this is likely to be in the focus at areas where this may be relevant).

In most instances warnings are phrased in a negative manner, i.e. "do not".

In many cases the safety and security information is "hidden" behind other information that markets the destiny. This is understandable, but in some cases navigating to find such information is difficult. Note – this is not a phenomenon unique only to South African tourism authorities/associations.

There is, with the exception of the provision of emergency numbers, virtually no advice on how to respond to various types of victimisation. In other words – if you have been a victim of card fraud, follow these steps, or if you had your passport stolen, then these are the steps.

Tourism Safety Initiative

The Tourism Safety Initiative (TSI) website provides information under two different sections – an open area, and a secure portal for clients. In the open area, general alerts and information on fraud prevention is displayed. There is also specific information for travelers and for businesses.

Analysis of SA

National Department of Tourism

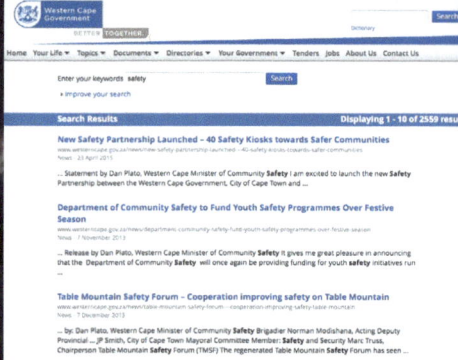

The NDT website lists issues relating to safety and security. Although reasonably comprehensive, there are a number of "don't's" or "not's", i.e. saying what tourist should not do, rather than what they should.

South African Tourism

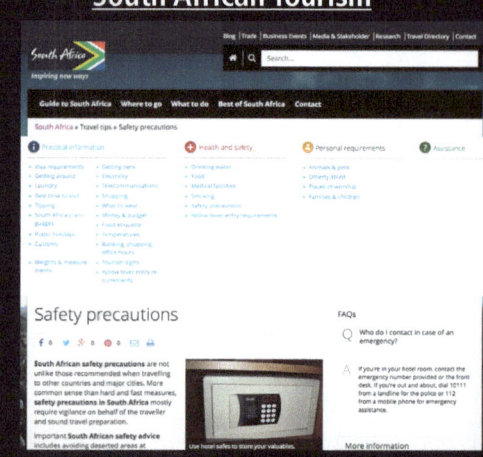

SAT's recommendations go under the guise of safety precautions and safety advice. In general these tips, albeit short, tend to have a positive message/tone.

WAY FORWARD

Through the Tourism Safety Initiative approach of focusing on establishing Public-Private Partnerships, the idea is for the industry to ultimately achieve the following:

Developing a common "macro" message that can be replicated at the level of South African Tourism, Tourism Business Council of South Africa, provincial and city levels.

From this generic message, more specific messages may be developed by local authorities, tourism product owners and service providers, etc.

These messages should in all cases phrase matters, as far as is possible, in a positive manner, i.e. "do" instead of "do not". Look at SABRIC as potential best practice.

Links would be provided of support of various types on all sites, i.e. emergency responders, trauma councillors, translators, embassies, banks, etc.

We will also develop common ways to respond to specific types of emergencies, especially under the categories of violent crime, fraud, extortion, and health and safety. This can be done with simple flow charts.

Through the TSI, a facility will be developed with the capabilities of responding to emergency needs of tourist travelling within the boundaries of South Africa as a destination.

These things should be developed in a "fun" manner, i.e. interactive colourful posters that integrate normal tourism information with safety and security information in a seamless manner.

In the final analysis, we recognise that what is required here is a joint, integrated strategy on how to handle the communication of safety and security messages horizontally and vertically throughout the tourism spectrum in a fused public and private sector approach.

This after all, the long term objectives of the TSI with the support of both the public sector at all levels and the private sector. **t**

Websites that Deal with Tourism Safety

Gauteng Tourism Authority

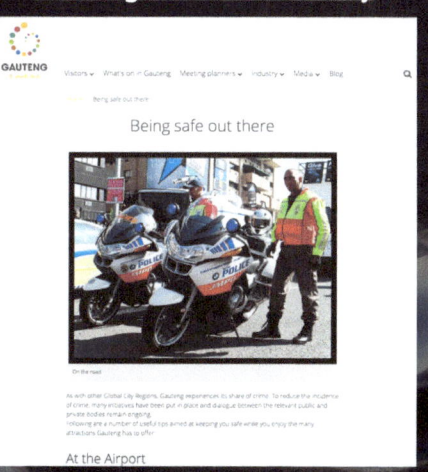

These tend to mirror the NDT ones to quite a large extent. There is also a great deal of focus on "don't" and "not".

Tourism KwaZulu-Natal

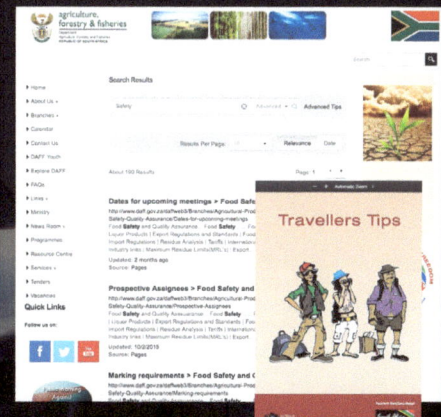

The KZN information is also displayed in a colourful flyer, with mostly the same information as in the others. In general quite pleasantly phrased and displayed.

South African Police Services

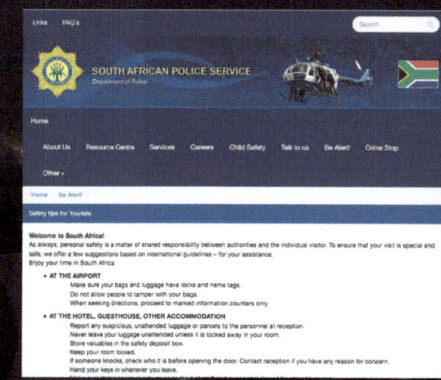

Safety information is provided for: the airport; the accommodation facility – quite comprehensive; On the street – quite comprehensive; In the vehicle; On hiking trails; and useful telephone numbers. Generally framed in a positive manner.

Western Cape Tourism

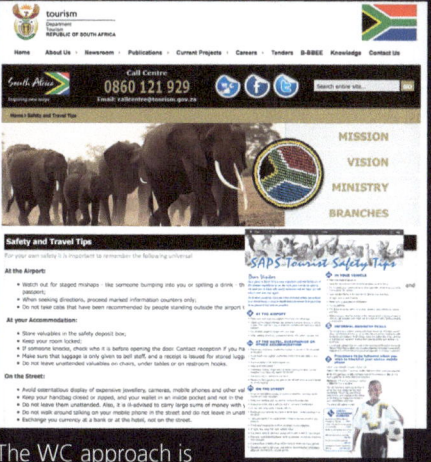

The WC approach is different as they encapsulate the messages in a brochure format. Also a great deal of focus on "don't" and "not".

Joburg Tourism

Only high level safety advice, as well as emergency numbers. The site itself provides very little and the focus is on marketing the destiny.

SABRIC

The South African Banking Risk Information Centre (SABRIC), although not a tourism entity, does display crime-related information. The difference is of course that SABRIC's core business is fighting crime. They have however managed to change their phraseology into a positive manger.